# The Story of

# Imelda Lambertini

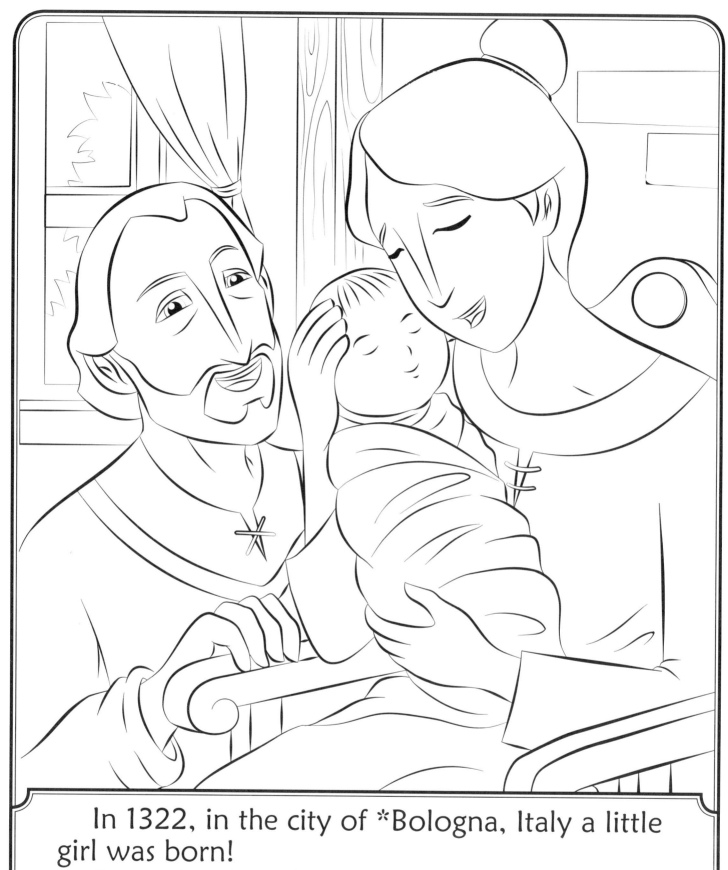

In 1322, in the city of *Bologna, Italy a little girl was born!

From the time she was very small, Imelda's parents taught her about God and how to pray.

*(Pronounced: bo-lo-nya)

Imelda loved God.
"Even though I am very young, show me
how I can serve You," she prayed.

Imelda's parents were aware of her love for God. But they were very surprised, when at 10 years old, she shared her heart's desire.

"I would like to serve God with the Dominican Sisters!" she said.

It was not an easy decision for Imelda's parents. She was their only child, and they loved her very much. Nevertheless, they prayed for God to show them what to do.

One day they sat down with Imelda.
"We love you very much, dear daughter,"
her father said, "but we <u>also</u> believe God is
calling you."

What a sacrifice Imelda and her parents made!
But in their hearts, they trusted God fully.

Even though Imelda was very happy in the convent, one thing made her quite sad.

"Reverend Mother," she said one day. "I want so much to receive Jesus in the Eucharist. May I join you and the other sisters when you have communion?"

The Mother Superior was very touched by Imelda's love of God, but in those days children younger than 12 were not allowed to receive Holy Communion.

"I'm sorry Imelda, you will have to wait a little longer," the Reverend Mother said. "But you may always adore Jesus in the Eucharist and make a spiritual communion."

Rather than let discouragement get the best of her, Imelda made her way to the chapel and knelt in prayer.

"Lord," she prayed, "I know I cannot have You now, but I want You to know that You can have all of me!"

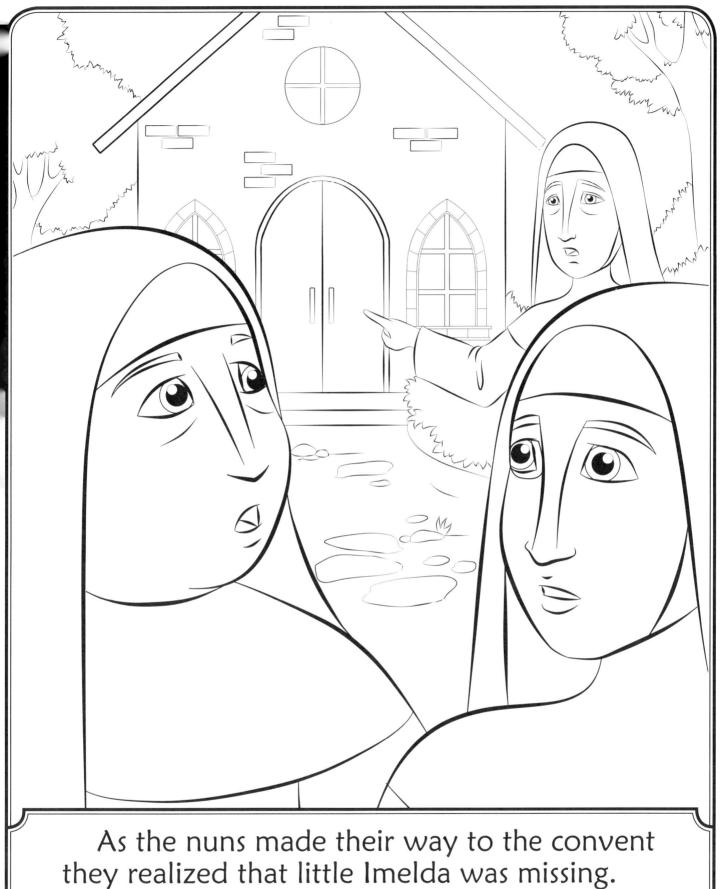

As the nuns made their way to the convent
they realized that little Imelda was missing.
"She must still be in the chapel," said one of
the nuns. "She loves to pray there."

The sisters opened the chapel doors and just as they had expected, Imelda was kneeling in prayer.

But there was something else they hadn't expected to see.

Right in front of little Imelda, a host was floating in the air. Jesus had come to Imelda!

Soon a priest was called. He carefully took hold of the sacred host and offered it to Imelda who partook of Jesus with a joyful and grateful heart!

Imelda was so happy! Even though others thought she was too young to partake of communion, Jesus didn't think so, and offered Himself to her in a very special way!

Blessed Imelda Lambertini is the Patroness of First Holy Communicants. Imelda was beatified by Pope Leo XII in 1826. Her feast day is May 13.